This Walker book belongs to:

____

____

For my girls and lovely Anna

– ZL

For Leon Wall

– AP

Florence & Fox

The Pet Mouse

Zanni Louise & Anna Pignataro

WALKER BOOKS
AND SUBSIDIARIES
LONDON • BOSTON • SYDNEY • AUCKLAND

'I have something good to tell you, Florence,' says Fox.

Florence knows what Fox is going to say. Fox is going to say he can do a handstand. Florence can already do handstands.

'I have a pet mouse,' says Fox.

This is not what Florence was thinking.

'Do you want to see him?' asks Fox.

'Sorry, Fox. I need to tidy my room,' says Florence, who never tidies her room.

At dinner, Florence asks her mum about mice. Florence's mum does not like mice.

'I am going to cross my fingers,' says Florence, 'and wish for a pet mouse.'

It is hard to eat spaghetti with crossed fingers. But Florence really wants a pet mouse.

When Florence wakes up in the morning, there is no mouse. Florence crosses her fingers and her toes.

It is hard to walk with crossed toes.

Florence doesn't mind hard.

She walks all day
with crossed toes
and crossed fingers.

But in the morning, there is still no pet mouse.

Florence crosses her fingers, toes and arms.

It is hard to dig holes with crossed fingers, toes and arms.

Actually, it is impossible.

'What's wrong?' asks Fox.

'Nothing is wrong,' says Florence.
'I am wishing for a pet mouse.'

But in the morning,
Florence does not
have a mouse.

She crosses her fingers,
toes, arms and legs.

She cannot do anything now. Florence hopes all this crossing works.

She also hopes Fox comes to visit because she cannot visit Fox. Maybe he will bring his pet mouse.

Fox does bring his mouse.

His mouse's name is Nick, and Nick likes celery.

Florence wonders whether Nick likes handstands too. He might not know about handstands because Fox is not very good at them.

Florence uncrosses everything and does a very good handstand for Nick. Nick looks impressed.

So does Fox.

'I wish I could do handstands,' says Fox.

'Cross your fingers,' says Florence. 'It might help.'

Florence and Fox: The Pet Mouse
first published in 2024
by Walker Books Australia Pty Ltd
Gadigal and Wangal Country
Locked Bag 22, Newtown
NSW 2042 Australia
www.walkerbooks.com.au

This edition published in 2025

Walker Books Australia acknowledges the Traditional Owners of the country on which we work, the Gadigal and Wangal peoples of the Eora Nation, and recognises their continuing connection to the land, waters and culture. We pay our respect to their Elders past and present.

NATIONAL LIBRARY OF AUSTRALIA
A catalogue record for this book is available from the National Library of Australia

ISBN: 978 1 761601 76 7

The illustrations for this book were created with pencil, coloured pencil, watercolour and collage.
Typeset in Caslon AntiqueVari
Printed and bound in China

EU Authorized Representative: HackettFlynn Ltd, 36 Cloch Choirneal, Balrothery, Co. Dublin, K32 C942, Ireland. EU@walkerpublishinggroup.com

10 9 8 7 6 5 4 3 2 1